I'M DONE BEING BROKEN

BROKEN

A Self-Healing Workbook

by

Antwoinette L. Ayers

TABLE OF *contents*

God, my God,
I yelled for help and
you put me together.
God, you pulled me
out of the grave,
gave me another chance at life
when I was down-and-out.

PSALM 30:2-3 MSG

Dedication

To my son whom I esteem to be a better version of me and whose name means to flow through unchartered territories. Nothing is exempt for you! I love you my blessed child with my whole life!

To my twelve nieces and nephews I'm trying my best to make sure you understand my sisters and I are doing our very best. To the best of our ability.

To my sisters, I love you for understanding and respecting my truth. This has not been an easy road but by faith we can get through everything. I never want to make you all uncomfortable. I only want to be free from guilt, shame and fear.

Asia and Brittany, may we grow and bond fruitfully.

To my dad and mother, thank you for giving me my life. May truth and healing take place for us all.

To my friends and loved ones, I've lost a lot and thank you for the grace you have given me. Please continue to add to my value, and I promise I will continue to encourage you to achieve higher.

To my Guardian Angels Prince Ella Ayers and Clancie Ree Hodges, I'm only a well to do woman because I was raised by brilliance and God's grace. The sacrifice you two made for me are the miracles I see now when I wake up. I get up daily to make you two proud. I miss you two dearly.

To my spiritual mothers. Thank you for healing the spots that ached in me for years. I owe to you the best representation of womanhood I can show.

To Courtney Ward Sr. Thank you for filling in as my dad when I couldn't reach or see mine. You are one of my heroes!

Introduction

Life experiences of highs and lows and suffering from chronic depression kept me oppressed for over 20 years. I suffered all forms of abuse. I had twin sisters named abandonment and rejection tagging along wherever I went. Eventually, my rebellion and bad choices ended up working in my favor and God allowed me to see my familiar as strange. I started seeing things differently. It forced me to dive into the anatomy of my purpose: sharing my story and writing this book.

When I first started writing, I felt scared, nauseated, and ashamed. I honestly attempted to throw it away several times. The fear and anxiety of "What are people going to say about me? " kept rushing through my mind. As much as I believe it's my calling to tell my story of how to break free, the voices of doubt were still very present.

The interesting thing about God and His voice of truth is that no matter how unsettled I was, I was still determined to write. Even when I'm afraid, there is something about doing things that shifts me into a woman of bold truth and courageous faith.

I wrote this book for the broken spirit who was robbed of their innocence. The peculiar soul who is ashamed to express their thoughts and creativity to the world. The battered spirit who finds it difficult to explain why they continued to love those who abused them and left them scarred.

I wrote this book for the rejected ones whose only hope is to be loved. For the ones who are tired of hearing the sabotaging voice of their past experiences speak louder than God's promises. I wrote this book for that person who wants to give up on life, whose every feeling is operating in the negative, and who seems to be fighting at every turn, including who they can turn to and who they can trust.

This book is for the person who needs to know how they can break free and walk in their healing and purpose.

Introduction

My story is not everybody's story, but if you can relate to what I described above, then this book is for you. Before you get started reading, writing and mediating over the next few pages, I want you to know three things:

1. You are a victor! You are no longer a slave to your past, toxic people, or the horrible situations you experienced. "Therefore, you are no longer a slave, but a son (daughter); and if a son (daughter), then an heir of God through Christ. " Galatians 4:7

2. You can be whole and have joy and peace! "May the God of hope fill you with all joy and peace as you trust in him, so that you may overflow with hope by the power of the Holy Spirit. " Romans 15:13

3. You are healed! "But he was pierced for our transgressions, he was crushed for our iniquities; the punishment that brought us peace was on him, and by his wounds we are healed." Isaiah 53:4-5

For every page written, I prayed and meditated over it. I pray that you allow this book to push you through the darkness you've been comfortable sitting in and run into your winning season full of light and restoration.

 Declare this over yourself: "I'm done being broken! I will walk in full authority of dominion and power today and the rest of my life.

"Whatever I have, wherever I am, I can make it through anything in the One who makes me who I am." Philippians 4:13 MSG

It's Time to Be Healed

You're not broken. But it's time for you to be healed.

From all the temptations you consumed by desires offered by false hope,

it's time for you to be healed.

From all the manic trauma introduced to your mind to steer you away from your destiny,

it's time for you to be healed.

From every loss and lost battle that forced you to dig in the depths of your reality and find out how to piece together peace,

it's time for you to be healed.

From every cycle of turmoil that fulfilled you in a misplaced season,

it's time for you to be healed.

From every real thing that turned out to be counterfeit,

it's time for you to be healed.

From all your droughts of emptiness,

it's time for you to be healed.

From all your pain and trials of suffering,

it's time for you to be healed.

From every ill and illegal word spoken over your life,

it's time for you to be healed.

From every broken scar hidden in the awkward parts of your past,

it's time for you to be healed.

From every mistake that you've made,

it's time for you to be healed.

I declare and decree that you will remove yourself from every broken place and position yourself to hear the Word of God and be healed from this moment forward.

Nature vs. Nurturer

The simplest definition of a nurturer is someone to help you develop and grow. In sociology class, I studied the difference between nature and nurture. Nature is the genetic makeup for a human, like being born a female or a male, brown eyes or blue eyes. Nurture is the influence of your surroundings, like how you were cared for, which determines how you grow and function in an environment.

In class, I was introduced to Harlow's Monkey experiment. In the experiment, Harlow separated infant monkeys from their biological mothers within 6 to 12 hours after birth. He then placed these baby monkeys in a nursery with "fake" mothers. One fake mother was made of wire mesh that did not have any soft surface. The other fake mother was made from wood that was covered in a terry cloth that was soft to touch and appeared to be cuddly.

After observing the baby monkeys over time, Harlow found that even though the baby monkeys received nourishment from both fake mothers, the baby monkeys still spent more time hugging on the terry cloth mother. This experiment showed that the bond between mother and infant was not solely based on whether the mother provided the baby monkey with physiological needs.

When faced with a stressful or threatening situation, the baby monkeys who had the terry cloth mother, would stay close and cuddle with it until they were calm. However, the baby monkeys who had the wire mesh mothers experienced the same stressful and threatening situations and would throw themselves on the floor and rock back and forth. These baby monkeys would not seek the wire mesh mother for comfort.

Harlow's Monkey experiment reinforced the importance of a mother-and-child bond, even as it relates to human babies. His theory believed that the establishment between a baby and mother is not only dependent upon their physiological needs (warmth, safety, food), but also their emotional needs (acceptance, love, affection). Both "fake" mothers provided food, but only one mother, the terry cloth one, provided comfort.

Nature vs. Nurturer

I share this experiment because it explained a lot to me on a personal level. I grew up with my mother and her husband. But at her house, I experienced sexual abuse by my stepfather. My mother cared for me like the wire mesh monkey, but she didn't provide me with comfort or security like the terry cloth monkey.

Due to the severity of the situation, I was abruptly pulled from my mother's home and made to go live with my grandmother. At the time, my grandmother was a senior citizen, but she ended up giving me the comfort I so desperately needed. Feeling as if I did something wrong, I began to carry rejection in my heart. For
years, I did not understand why the one person I needed the most couldn't console me. Especially after finding out her husband was a predator to an innocent child she birthed.

Instead, my grandmother became my safe haven. She was the one who showed me how to dress. She taught me how to address people in the room. How to respect and honor your mother and father as unto the Lord. She spoke the words of the Bible to me before I even knew what the Bible was. Honestly, as much as she tried to guide me, my heart was having trouble receiving from her because I thought by nature, my mother was supposed to teach me and nurture me.

Unfortunately, it wasn't until my grandmother passed away, I realized that although some women may carry a child, it does not make them a mother. God didn't replace my mother – she carried me; instead, God blessed me with my grandmother who became my legal guardian. It was through her that I experienced and understood what it meant to love, and be loved, unconditionally. God still needs both women to do their part, so I can do what He has predestined me to do. The more I matured in my life journey, the more I understood this.

Nature vs. Nurturer

Personally, I believe the enemy tried to destroy me as a little girl. His direct assignment was to make me feel invaluable and to withdraw love from me. As a child growing up without a mother or a father within my physical reach, I had an identity crisis. However, over time through years of expensive therapy and studying lessons on forgiveness, I was able to journal my thoughts and understand myself and my mother's place in my life.

As a pre-teen and even through my adulthood years, I struggled with a child-like mindset. Due to this trauma, I was unable to convey my thoughts and emotions of my behavior. I believe children who lived with unresolved pain, overlooked offenses by loved ones and anger from something they experienced while growing up, can be subjective to live in that child-like mindset for years. From the outside, we witness them grow up physically, but internally, they are still trapped in that pain mentally from the hurt they endured in the past.

But God, in His timing will use the people around you to give you exactly what you need. Whoever didn't nurture you, in the way you felt like they should have, God will fill that void. When I needed guidance from a male perspective, my older cousin was there to help me. When I wanted to travel out of town, and my granny was unable to take me, my church stepped in and took us everywhere. The things most parents did with their children, I was still able to do, just differently.

God still provided experiences for me, even though I still wondered and asked, "Why didn't my mother or father protect me?" As I matured in my faith, I started analyzing how God was processing me to know Him as God! All the while, He was restoring what I felt I lacked in my life. I didn't realize that God had sent my grandmother to help guide and nurture me. Mainly, because I was too busy being blinded by my mother's rejection, the physical absence of my father and her husband who abused me.

Nature vs. Nurturer

I'm sure there have been plenty of times when you dismissed help or love of someone else. Either you were offended unintentionally, or you rationalized within yourself that you didn't need the help or didn't deserve it. Your past hurt wouldn't allow you to trust anyone. The truth is, hurt and pain brings the desire for someone else to make us feel good about ourselves for a moment. We try to reason with our pain. However, it becomes your responsibility to stop addressing the hurt with blame. Instead, trade in the will to stay angry and call on God to live whole and free.

I found my healing and freedom after reading Titus 2:3-5. It changed my perspective on how I viewed my mother and what I thought I needed from her; God gave it to me in the form of my grandmother who was not even biologically related to me. God gave me a Guardian angel! That's better than the terry cloth mother!

"Likewise, teach the older women to be reverent in the way they live, not to be slanderers or addicted to much wine, but to teach what is good. Then they can urge the younger women to love their husbands and children, to be self-controlled and pure, to be busy at home, to be kind, and to be subject to their husbands, so that no one will malign the word of God." Titus 2: 3-5

As you answer these questions, reflect on what you've learned about yourself, channeling any issues you may have encountered with other women. It's okay to feel sad, hurt and confused as you do this work, but it's necessary to discover the pain from those relationships. Relationships with women are not easy, especially when you have mother issues. We often hear about daddy issues, but it's a different kind of pain when it's from the one who births you. Partly because that's your connection to your greatest tribe of women. You are the woman that you see in other women. I encourage you to break the curse by giving other women the love and nurture you needed.

Nature vs. Nurturer

Maybe some of you experienced abuse, lack of attention or nurturing, or had a mother who was too strong. Whatever the situation is, explore each question and write out how they make you feel and what feelings you think were birthed from those experiences.

Here is a list of questions that I believe will help you address and channel some of your past hurt with women. The path towards healing requires us to dig deep into our rooted issues to figure out what we've lacked from women. Realizing what we've lack will allow us to address those issues in your life now.

- What type of relationship do you have with your mother?
- Who is the woman in your life that has been like a mother to you?
- Are you willing to be steered by another woman? If not, why?
- Can you forgive your mother without ever bringing up what happened in your past?
- Can your mother correct you? Can you accept it?
- Can you talk to your mother about everything? Why not?
- Do you feel offended by your mother? Why can't you get over these offenses?
- Can you share your deepest darkest secrets with your mother/mother figure?
- Do you have issues celebrating another woman's success? Why?
- Are you, or can you, be a nurturer to your children?
- What did you feel you lack as a woman?
- Are you a woman you can look up to? If not, how can you change that?

Nature vs. Nurturer

Use this space to answer the questions from above.

Nature vs. Nurturer

Nature vs. Nurturer

Nature vs. Nurturer

Dear God,

Reveal the woman in my life that you have assigned to me to help shape me into the full masterpiece you have called me to be! Help me see that she is not my enemy or competition. Help me to receive correction from her, even if I disagree with it. Soften my heart so I can be reminded by her how valuable I am to this world. Help us both see each other as equals and encourage us to keep striving to be better. Lord I thank you for her, in advance for being a blessing to me. In return God, cover her and fulfill her glory days with an outcry of love and appreciation.

In Jesus name, amen.

Insecurity

Insecurity was a deep-rooted issue for me. Having a dark chocolate complexion, crooked teeth, and scarred skin, I never considered myself pretty. Although I was never called ugly, I couldn't see what others saw in me. My insecurity was rooted in having to live behind the secrets of being molested by my stepfather. Wondering, was it normal? To be a little girl and sexually pleasing a grown man. Every time I was in trouble, that was his means of punishment for me. Had other girls gone through it too? Why me? These were the questions I always wondered.

I always felt so alone because no one close to me talked about this evil crime. It was so passive in all communities and so I hid behind it. Not knowing I was shrinking in more areas of my growth. I couldn't see pass the filth that I had been exposed to, and it blinded me. Consequently, as I grew older, I became promiscuous.

I got into relationships with different men after naively being swept up by their charm. It wasn't until it was too late that I realized some of these men had seen my insecurities and played on them. Some even used it against me. I remembered telling one of my exes what happened to me when I was a child and he responded, "A man told me never to get with a woman who has been sexually violated or molested. " I felt like an idiot for sharing my darkest secret with him.

It was to the point in that relationship with that same ex, I had to break down in detail what happened to me, so he could understand why sexually I couldn't do that one thing he desired so adamantly from me. I couldn't perform oral sex on him because of the man who forced himself on me as a child. The more I lived with my disgust and fear, I felt even more worthless having to explain my "no" to someone who said they loved me. I lived with the guilt of abuse from my past for so long, it was beginning to hunt me in my present. My ex at the time still couldn't understand even after I explained my childhood horror. He was very demanding in this sexual act. He even told me, "No man would want to be with me if I thought I wasn't going to give him head." The enemy once again had crept into my life coming after my deepest darkest wound disguised as the person I thought I needed and loved.

Insecurity

I cried out to God, begging him to help me see my strengths. I prayed to God daily to show me how to undo this agony my heart had endured. My insecurities were so deeply rooted from so many experiences, that I became weak. Seeking attention in areas that were so toxic to my soul. Sex toys at one point were my go-to for relief. There was no physical harm in that, and no one knew my business. So, it was valid in my eyes and it kept me from having my name in the streets. I realized I was using other things to give me the physical feeling of the undescribed emotions I needed.

For this reason, I had to get an understanding of who I am and what God said about my worth. I asked God to show me how beautiful and worthy I was, and will remain, in His eyes. I was tired of looking at myself with disappointment, acting foolish, having resentment and anger because I kept wanting others to see that I was the prize. I yearned for men to see my beauty and to see past my scars. I desired to be loved so badly by these men, that I was willing to do anything to make them happy. I was so broken, that even at the expense of losing myself, I was willing to exchange it longing for their love.

Insecurities can be invitations sent to rob you of your worthiness. They set up false accusations that make you believe that others see them, but they don't. They are birthed from what you allowed yourself to believe about the pain inflicted on you. No one could explain why inhumane things happen to innocent people. This is only an area where the devil himself gains compliments, but only God can reveal and heal.

Insecurities will keep you in a paranoid state causing you to sit in isolation, feeling depressed and empty. Insecurities are lies set up as false presentations to keep you blind to the hurt that brought you to broken places in your life. They play on your mind. They keep you in a constant wonder of, "Is this for me? Do I deserve this? " The voices of doubt, insecurity, and unworthiness are lies from the enemy and your past.

Insecurity

Examples of insecurities can include things, like you having to talk about yourself before someone else says something about you or you overly explaining yourself and why you do it. Insecurities are like warning signs that you tell people about yourself, without them asking for it. Insecurities secure your will to stay lost in your identity of self.

With insecure characteristics, you might even become aggressive because you want total control over how others treat you. You try and put a front up as if you are this big bad wolf, but the moment someone says something to you out the way, it will crush you to tears. Insecurities are hidden behind a person's invisible wall. It's like a game: you want to be seen and then when it works against you, you don't want anyone to see them.

Social media has made it quite easy to live a comfortable, insecure life. We live behind a computer and create a fake, unrealistic world that sees us living our "best life," but when it's time to step out onto the platform, we sink in the spotlight and our insecurities are revealed. We talk a good game, but we never win the victory because we have not mastered what has mastered us, our insecurities. We look good on social media, but we are broken on the inside. We try to sound intelligent but can't speak to people on a common level of normalcy because the pursuit of being significant hides us from our eternal issues.

I have also witnessed people become very passive when they don't understand how insecure they are. Insecurities can sometimes open doors for people to misuse you. People can see when you don't fully know who you are, and they will prey on that. Insecurity is a silent identity killer that can keep you complacent and subjected to hurt. Going forward we will agree it's time for you to deny your insecurities, boldly and loudly.

When God created every human being, he knew that we would have challenges in this life. However, from the beginning, He gives us clear instructions in scripture to be bold and courageous.

Insecurity

Being bold and courageous is the opposite of insecurity and fear. It opens your mind to new perspectives and allows your heart to be led unapologetically by transparency. Gaining a sense of who you are and learning to celebrate overcoming the brokenness you were once bounded to, will alter your mind into acceptance and peace.

"The simple believes every word, But the prudent considers well his steps.
A wise man fears and departs from evil, but a fool rages and is self- confident."
Proverbs 14:15-16

It is important to identify the root cause of your insecurities from your past experiences. I hope by answering these questions truthfully, it will help you get to the bottom of your pain so you can experience a breakthrough.

- Write down a list of your biggest insecurities?
- Where do you think these insecurities came from?
- Are you controlling? Aggressive? Or passive because of them?
- Write about a time when you did something that was out of your character because of your insecurity.
- Can you name other people who played on your insecurities and how it made you feel?
- Have you evaluated your friends and family to see if they contribute to your insecurities?
- Have you prayed to God and asked him to help you? Why or why not?
- For the people who've hurt you, have you forgiven them? And moved on from them?
- Do you believe in yourself? Or do you continue to allow yourself to be hurt because of your insecurities?
- What do you think you can do right now to release yourself from the bondage of insecurity?

Insecurity

Use this space to answer the questions from above.

Insecurity

Insecurity

Insecurity

Dear God,

Help me believe and receive who you created me to be. Help me to remove the words that fed into my insecurities and vulnerability. Help me understand that every negative word spoken over me was not ordained by your love. Forgive me for the times I acted foolish because I was ensnared into believing I had to show revenge to those who hurt me. Help me with my insecurities and thank you for sending your son to help me with my unbelief. I am a new creature because of your great grace and that is enough for me and even those that tried to harm me. Help me to embrace every word you said about me. Replace my weakness with your strength and my insecurities with your powered confidence.

In Jesus name, amen.

Daddy Issues

My dad always gave me sound advice, but he never lived up to the wise words that he spoke from my perspective. There were a lot of things I needed from him, yet I never received them. He was out of town most of my life and because of that he couldn't teach me the lessons I needed from my father. So, unfortunately, I became a scholar based upon my own experiences.

It is a huge blessing to a little girl to have a dedicated father who can protect her and give her wise counsel as she grows up. It doesn't matter what role a man plays in her life, as a woman it is our inherent desire to want them to protect us. No matter if the man is a father, uncle, brother, or cousin, , they are expected to protect the women in their life when they reach a certain age.

Satan is very cunning in this area. He likes to rob little girls of their earthly father, who is supposed to resemble God. When a girl has been raised by her father, she has the privilege to have him through every struggle. When things become difficult, he is there to steer her back in the right direction.

Little girls like me who grew up with just a woman, I didn't realize how much not having a physical father presence impacted my life. I didn't know how much I needed a dad until I wrote down every man's name that I had been with and what I liked about them. Then I wrote down everything I liked about my daddy and what I wished he had taught me. When I compared the two lists, I almost threw up! The character traits that I lacked from my dad, I found in each of the men I had some type of relationship with.

I felt so sick seeing myself revealed like that. This was a simple exercise assigned by my therapist and it was shocking how much I relied on other men, simply because my dad wasn't around. In my life I lacked the things that only a father could provide. This realization was detoxing for me. I was waking up to everything that I was using to fill the void of my father's absence.

Daddy Issues

Don't get me wrong, my dad gave me what he could. He tried his best. Thankfully, my grandmother and grandfather helped me see how a girl/woman should be treated. As I grew older, I began to understand and channel the advice my grandfather had spoken to me, "treat her like a lady."

I was glad that my grandfather was there for a short time in my life. I not only got to see a long-lasting marriage, but I enjoyed listening to him talk about life. My grandfather showed me simple pleasures in life that meant a lot to me, he really treated me like a lady by opening the door for me and taking me occasionally to get special treats. I felt like a princess with him.

"You shall not afflict any widow or fatherless child. If you afflict them in any way, and they cry at all to Me, I will surely hear their cry. " Exodus 22:22

Sometimes we women struggle with how we are supposed to be treated mentally and physically when our natural fathers don't show us how to receive proper love. Many times, it's like a girl without a father figure becomes unaware of how a man is supposed to treat her. We search with no guidance on what we think a decent man should be. After a while, we start to lose hope because our standard of a what man is or what a man is supposed to do, is developed from our experiences with men. Which, if you are like me, aren't great examples. Suffering from the hurt of an absentee father or long-distance father-daughter relationship, causes us to have a challenging time respecting men and trusting them.

I believe this is one of the reasons why we must invest in therapy to help us develop healthy coping skills for dating and for life. As well as having a few accountable friends that we feel comfortable sharing our dating experiences with. The goal is to not encounter the same mistakes that our daddy issues led us to, but to learn and deal with the real issue.

Daddy Issues

My prayer is that every little girl has someone to open the door for them and remind them of how beautiful they are without compromising their innocence or dignity. Those small moments of time and my grandfather's mannerisms influenced the tone of how worthy I am for the right man to pay attention to me. I used those memories to help me remember that I'm supposed to be treated with respect and honor. Even though my real father was absent, the example he set for me helped me become the entrepreneur, defender and scholar that I am now.

I hope these questions channel any daddy issues you may have. Allow yourself to feel what you feel and cry if necessary. Grief and burdens are heavy, but when you pull back the layers of what your daddy did or did not do in your life, real change happens. Use these questions to allow your perspectives to be opened to finally receive the respect from the men in your life, both now and later.

- Do you have a father figure? If not, what did you feel you missed out on?
- Do you attract the wrong type of men because of it?
- Is your father a role model for your husband or son? Is your husband a good role model?
- Do you have a spiritual Father you trust? A pastor, deacon, etc. who pray for you?
- Have the men in your life been an abuser or a protector? Explain how.
- If your father was absent or semi-absent, can you make peace with him?
- Compare and contrast the men you dated with the traits of your father.
- What do you wish your father could have taught you?
- Do you have trust issues with men?
- If you aren't married, what characteristics would you like for him to have?
- How can you give your children a better relationship with father figures in their life?

Daddy Issues

Use this space to answer the questions from above.

Daddy Issues

Daddy Issues

Daddy Issues

Dear God,

My father was not able to give me the tools I needed to understand a man's love. I believe he did his best, regardless if I knew him or not. God, I believe and know that you are my true Father, no matter what I experienced. Teach me why the Lord is my shepherd and why I lack nothing. Help me not to seek other men to fill in the gaps of what I feel like I lacked with my earthly father. Lord, guide me, protect me and teach me. Help me to be led by your spirit and become confident and aware of situations. Please Lord don't allow me to be led by my daddy issues, my vulnerability, or low confidence. I trust you and I put my confidence and hope in you.

In Jesus name, Amen

Bitterness

One of the side effects of rejection, abandonment and insecurity is bitterness. Bitterness means having or expressing anger and disappointment at being mistreated or having resentment. It was such a profound revelation to me when I discovered how bitter I was. It wasn't that I was intentionally trying to be bitter because of what happened to me as a little girl, it was just a quality that I picked up over the years because of the rejection, abandonment and insecurities I suffered.

It wasn't my attitude so much; it was how I viewed my life based on the cultural norm of children being raised by a mother and a father, or at least one of their parents. That wasn't my story, and I did not like it, especially with both parents being alive and well. That was a bitter cup for me. The devil was very crafty with his attempt to steal my joy.

As I grew spiritually, I noticed that his assignment was to get me to gravitate towards the negative encounters of what impacted my childhood. Satan had to come after me when I was a child. The foundation of a child's mind is critical to how we view life, opinions, and thoughts because it's all governed by familiarity. Essentially, Satan tried to rob me of my ability to have pure joy for the rest of my life. Knowing the enemy's main objective is to steal, kill and destroy. Satan had to kill my innocence when I was younger because joy keeps me in a relationship with God's perfect will for my life.

I was bitter at a young age on many levels in my mind. No one bothered to answer the whys I had or gave a reason to believe they were on my side. The more I thought about what happened to me as a child, the more I began to question myself. I was molested, separated from my mother and my sisters, and was sent to live with my grandmother, and I was too young to really comprehend it all. Eventually I grew to hate me. I started to think maybe I should have kept quiet and let whatever happen to me happen because I was dying on the inside once it came to light.

Bitterness

I hated who I was, and it reflected in my behavior as a child. I fought every year in middle school. Bitterness and anger were the unheard sounds behind every demerit ever wrote about me. It wasn't until I found someone who showed me that they cared for me, that my whole demeanor shifted. The joy of having someone who I felt was on my side, who loved me, created a balance from all my chaos. I didn't realize how rough I was until he told me. Everybody else would say I was bad or a troublemaker, but he would always defend me by saying, "She's been through a lot."

My bitterness began to shrink after being with someone who understood me. I fell in love with someone who saw me for me. This part of my life was so special and significant because it shifted me from bitterness to gaining the attention I longed for from somebody. Being young and in love, at the time, gave me a place to oppress my internal issues. However, that only sustained me for a limited of time before my bitterness found a way to attach itself to me again.

I ended up getting pregnant and having an abortion. I thought it was in the best interest for him, because he had such a promising future as an incredible athlete. Consequently, he broke up with me because he could not understand why I would do such a thing when he was willing to be a part of his child's life. He dumped me in my most divisive state of mind and heart. That scar on top of all the other scars became another badge of bitterness that haunted me for years. Leaving me wondering the possibilities of what could have been with my child and with him.

That child could have gone to college, or even better, could have grown up in a two-parent household. Being involved with that man, was one of the healthiest relationships I had ever been in. However, I wasn't the healthiest woman mentally or spiritually. Unfortunately, all those built-up scars started to become more roots of bitterness. Born out of that came the rebounds and the settling version of me, because I didn't know balance or how to let go of my issues.

Bitterness

I've since realized that bitterness is a silent seed. Most times, bitter people don't even know they're bitter. In their minds, they probably just think they are mad, like always. Signs of bitter people, I've discovered, are that they hold grudges, are jealous, struggle to accept advice, and don't seek to make changes to better themselves.

Bitterness solidifies your why and the way you think. Unlike being mad, which you eventually let go of, bitterness stays with you and you end up being impacted by it. For example, if I loan you money and you don't pay it back, I will be mad, and I probably won't ever loan money to you again. However, I might loan someone else money with no problem. But bitterness says I loaned you money, you never paid it back, and now going forward no one can ever borrow money from me again. I've created a wall, all because of what one person did.

Creating walls like that creates bitterness. It becomes rooted inside you and it lives outside you and everyone and anyone you encounter is impacted by it. Bitterness attaches itself to the scars of what you endured, and it rarely lets us go.

I didn't know how bitter I was at my mom, dad and everybody around me until I realize people didn't want to be around me. I was paranoid by hearing people talk about how angry or foolish I was. Therapist after therapist taught me how to handle my anger. I just decided I didn't want to live and do life like this anymore. I wasn't happy and it was eating me up inside. I was hurting outwardly so much I couldn't see it. Being tormented in my mind night and day with questions no one could answer was the result of so much resentment. People that were supposed to love and protect me, did the complete opposite. I made myself believe they hated me and as a result, I hated myself.

Bitterness

Bitterness had history with me without a doubt. I thank God for my Granny introducing me to God while she raised me. In return, I can use the Word to deliver me from bitterness. The more I started reading the word of God, the more healing and strength I acquired to get rid of all bitterness inside me. Not only reading the Bible, but I wrote a letter to everyone that hurt me. I asked God to help bring back all my pain so I could face it. I was tired of feeling like I was hiding and running from invisible prison walls. The word of God was the answer to my whys. I thought I desperately needed to hear from people the explanation of the questions I had, but I realized, all I needed and need, is God's word to comfort me.

Get rid of all bitterness, rage and anger, brawling, and slander, along with every form of malice. Be kind and compassionate to one another, forgiving each other, just as in Christ God forgave you. Ephesians 4:31

Answer the questions below to understand your issues with bitterness. Be honest with yourself and trust God to help you to recognize it and deliver you from it.

- Are you bitter/ or have you been bitter?
- What did your bitterness justify in your life?
- Has anyone told you were bitter?
- Are you resentful of certain people?
- Do you always seem to see a negative perspective first?
- Can you write down the names of people you are angry with?
- Can you forgive yourself for holding on to bitterness or grudges for so long?
- Are you ready to forgive without an apology?
- Do you have anger issues?
- Retrace your steps for the times you acted out angrily?
- Can you forgive yourself for living in bitterness?

Bitterness

Use this space to answer the questions from above.

Bitterness

Bitterness

Bitterness

Dear God,

Can you show me my heart? The pain of my past and issues now are causing me to live bitter. I no longer want to adapt to the lie Satan has been feeding me. I want to prosper in every divine will you have for my life. I want to experience the joy of your salvation that your son so freely gave. God please heal and reveal my heart issues so I can grow pass them. Let me use my past issues to minister to others. Let them be used to glorify your name and keep me in alignment with your healing and delivering my mind.

In Jesus name, Amen

 Suicide

As bad as it sounds, taking my life away seemed easier than living the life I was living. In my mind, suicide became the only thing that would take my worries away. I just thought the world would be better off without me in it. When you have suffered so much internal pain, we sometimes need to feel the physical form of pain to understand how we are feeling.

Inside I was bottled up with darkness and heartache, and not being able to "see" that hurt, was almost like a disappointment itself. How can we know we're hurting if we can't see it? You can see that someone is pretty, but you can't always see that they are hurting. I wanted people to see past my beauty and understand the pain and hurt I was experiencing.

We can experience a lot of trauma and never have the scars to prove it. If you tell the wrong people what you're struggling with, sometimes they'll even think you're making it up because it sounds so farfetched from normalcy. That in itself can create even more pain. For me, suicide just made sense.

With my mother placing me in my grandmother's care and my father being long distant, I never had a deep connection with them. I felt a huge void instead. Apart of me was dead already, it paralyzed my heart. I wanted to escape the pain. In my mind, no one cared or worried about me anyway, besides my grandmothers whom were elderly themselves. "Not being in pain anymore, problem solved," is what I often contemplated.

Every day for me was like living in suicide. I had to watch and listen to people that I love, not love me back. I would listen to my granny tell me stories about my mother and sisters doing this and that. My dad telling me about everything he was doing in out of town. Most holidays I was alone.

Suicide

As I got older, I was no longer excited about them, versus when I was a child, I had always looked forward to them. I remember many Christmases, looking out the window, wondering why people didn't come over my grandmother's house to wish us a Merry Christmas. It felt like my spirit died every time I didn't spend time with people, I thought I should have.

I was alone and I was poor. Not just in spirit, but financially too. I couldn't afford to do something because my grandmother didn't have the money, I broke down even more. I became good at guarding my pain and I mastered making it unnoticeable to my grandmother, as I understood that they did their best by me. I didn't want to ask anybody and couldn't ask anyone for help. I was a child, why did I have to call and tell adults what I needed for a love experience.

So, suicide made everything equal in my mind. It would have eliminated what I thought was the problem: me. Suicide starts as a seed, and if you're not careful, it can quickly take root and haunt you. I've made a lot of bad decisions, that in the moment, felt like good decisions, but those decisions can affect you long term if you let them. I remember laying across the abortion table and experiencing life being taken from my body.

When it was all said and done, I walked out realizing not only was my baby's life gone, but I was gone too. I was lost, confused, broken, and rotting away. I felt like a zombie. It was like I became so comfortable with death and pain, that I allowed it to put me in a coma of hurt. Feelings become thoughts and our thoughts become words.

We are in kinship with death in our subconscious mind when we feel pain. When we state we can't do something that is a red flag, we give up too early. Not realizing this slowly kills our hope and our potential. Likewise, that's how regrets are born. Instead of killing myself, I decided to kill the words I was speaking and the thoughts I was thinking about myself. Instead of speaking death, I began to speak life. Instead of thinking about my pain, I started confessing my hope in Christ Jesus.

Suicide

If you are on this level of healing a brokenness, the only things you need to kill, or abort is doubt, self-sabotage, low self-esteem, stinking thinking, and words that don't build up others. We must command our thoughts to switch from our negative experiences and make them positive.

Suicide is not necessarily evolved around death. Some of us commit suicide when we ignore what our instincts tell us. When the Holy Spirit warns us, that's a sign of love from him that we are about to embark on a detour that will cause some turbulence. When we ignore that gut feeling, that's suicide.

Not producing the creative genius in you is suicide. Not opening the business, you desire so badly, is suicide. Those are all forms of spiritual suicide. That's what we must be on the lookout for. Listening to that voice of purpose, while rejecting the loud sound of chaos. That will keep us going in the right direction.

Even down to the little things that make us feel defeated. Like when we spend money that we know we need for the bills, on trivial things like clothes or a new phone. When we do irrational things, it's only to satisfy temporary relief. Those little behaviors are the ones that we must get rid of. If it steals, kills or destroys you, that's not from God. Don't steal from yourself in the natural or in your mind.

Suicide

You owe yourself a new way of thinking. Be honest with yourself when you answer these questions. It's ok to tell yourself the truth and to forgive yourself. Facing this truth will help you heal going forward. Answer truthfully not worrying about judgment. This is your life. Save your life.

- Have you tried to commit suicide?
- Have you ever had an abortion?
- Have you ever been addicted to anything?
- How did you handle the aftermath of any of the above?
- Have you asked God to forgive you?
- Have you forgiven yourself?
- Have you self-sabotaged anything because you didn't think you were ready for it?
- What secrets are you hiding that you're embarrassed to share?
- Are you ashamed of your story?
- Do you think about dark things a lot? (Depression, death, paranoia, suicide, etc.)
- Do you hate someone? Do you hate yourself?
- What have you done to numb the pain you are experiencing?

Suicide

Use this space to answer the questions from above.

Suicide

Suicide

Suicide

Dear God,

I repent. Forgive me for every foul word I spoke over myself or someone else. Forgive me for killing things out of disobedience, ignorance and forgetting that you give grace and mercy. God I'm sorry I tried to kill myself physically and mentally, I didn't know the greatness that lives in me. God heal me from pain. Open my eyes to the beauty of my brokenness and show me the masterpiece you're molding me to be. Thank you for tossing my sins into the sea of forgiveness. Thank you that I am now free indeed! Jesus hold my hand and take the knife out of my past and switch it with the sword of your word.

In Jesus Name, Amen

If you're thinking about suicide, are worried about a friend or loved one, or would like emotional support, the Lifeline network is available 24/7 across the United States. Lifeline is available for everyone, and it's free and confidential.

National Suicide Prevention Lifeline
1-800-273-8255

Manipulation

I spent a lot of time as a young adult using sex as a tool to manipulate men into staying in a relationship with me. I believed that if I sexed a man in a particular way that he would never leave me because he wouldn't want to miss out on what I was offering between the sheets first and in my brain second. I believed that if I treated him like a king, he would never leave me. It was something about having a man, that made a difference in my life. I arrogantly knew I was the best and any man that had me was lucky to have me.

I had this strong need to be loved but the problem was, I was making the wrong people love me. I was always trying to make it fit, to make them love me because I deserved it. Looking back now, I realized I was in a sunken place trying to cope with my life's broken puzzle pieces. When I forcibly wanted love from people that could never love me with the full capacity I needed, I grew in selfish ambition. At the time I didn't know I was doing that. I just thought what I desired was right, and I was tired of being mishandled. With this mind, all the pain, hurt and manipulation grew into a sense of pride, control and aggression.

I knew I would be the woman these men needed even after the breakup. I was truly a game player in all my relationships. In most cases, I didn't get this way until after I saw that my heart was being taken for granted. I didn't start off with a manipulating spirit, it was awakened when I saw people taking my kindness for granted with intentions to not give it back.

I was loved from a broken heart, and I was determined to make sure I was going to be the best any man had ever had. Not knowing that I was setting myself up to be emptied on people who were still going to choose themselves. At the end of the day, I was still left broken emotionally and physically when all the men I had to have in my life, either walked away or I left them once destruction became our common love language. Consequently, that thrilled us more than the pursuit of God's love for a marriage.

Manipulation

Being married taught me one thing. Never think you are strong enough to handle what your husband can't. You must be willing to know everything is not worth fighting for. After experiencing all forms of abuse, I was determined not to have that happen to me again. So much so, I became aggressive even more in my actions to prove I am a good pick. I became so cocky about what I was and wasn't going to let happen, that I built this dynamic front to hide behind. We were fighting so much, that I allowed it to be normal.

I had plenty of solid friendships with my female friends, but I was off balance when it came to men. I was bargaining my worth with men, and I was forcing people to be in my life who didn't need to be there. The funny thing is they were in love with me, but I was forcing myself to love some of them. I didn't love them, I just lusted after them. I was exposed to the spirit of perversion as a child, so sex became a form of aggression and release for me.

For a while, it worked. But then sex became diluted and the real side of some of these men started to show. It was almost as if manipulation was attracting manipulation. The same tool I thought I hand control over, drove me in a deeper illusion out of the land of love. At one point I remember around age 16, homosexuality crossed my brain. My own internal thoughts were manipulating me and trying to find a connection of familiarity to stay traveling down the opposite road of God's word.

In my own mind I had already told myself that no one will ever hurt me again and I meant that. I didn't know the value of what I carried in my good areas. I kept holding on to lesser value things because I refused to be rejected by anyone else again.

Manipulation

I was searching for love in all the wrong places, I was like, "you are going to see me and love me!" no matter what. Then my son was born. My first true love and the purest form of unconditional love a woman could ever receive after years of failed relationships.

My son taught me that I didn't have to be who I was in order for those other men to love me. The moment I had him, I realized that I needed to change my thought process and all the negative traits that used to guide me in the wrong direction. I had to unlearn those negative patterns and choose to go in the right direction. His love caused me to see myself in a different light.

I realized I had to hold myself accountable with these characteristic traits flowing from manipulation. What made me think people were supposed to see me and love me when I couldn't see me or love me? Why did I desire something they couldn't even give themselves? I had to remind myself that I was a child of God. My son helped me to see that I was more than enough. God saw fit that he could trust me to raise a child. A son at that! I knew I was going to have a boy when I first found out I was pregnant. My child, my son, became the motivation for me to grow mentally and spiritually moving forward.

"Do nothing out of selfish ambition or vain conceit. Rather, in humility value others above yourselves, not looking to your own interests but each of you to the interests of the others." Philippians 2:2-4

Manipulation

It wasn't until I asked myself, "when am I going to allow myself to become a lady?" I had to understand that I did have a caring heart and not a cold spirit. If you're not careful, your past can muddy up your future. I allowed my past to make me aggressive. A twin brother to manipulation. Even though aggression is necessary at the right time and place, it took me some time to figure out when the necessary times are.

- Do you view yourself from the point of offense and aggression?
- Have you ever fought for something you never really wanted?
- Do you take pride in seeing other people's karma?
- Have you ever forced someone to see and/or to be with you?
- How do you respond to being rejected?
- Have you ever wanted to get revenge on someone who hurt you?
- How do you respond to fear?
- Have you been physically violent with people in your past?
- Have you ever wanted people to feel your pain?
- How do you release tension? Does this help keep you grounded?
- Explain why you have a wall up? Can this wall be torn by you? Or someone else?
- In what ways can you seek restoration?

Manipulation

Use this space to answer the questions from above.

Manipulation

Manipulation

Manipulation

Dear God,

Show me my aggressive and manipulative ways. Show me the ways in which I resist people because I'm scared to let them get too close to me. God show me how to be meek and mild. Show me how to speak gently in spirit and be aggressive in praying for others and coming before your presence. God settle my spirit in your wings so I can rest my fighting nature. Use my powerful force to instead war for your kingdom in the spirit realm. Help me to see you never intended for me to be hurt by the people I trusted. But show me Lord how to use my pain and past for the advancement of your kingdom. Let me be a vessel to help someone else heal in the same parts that once broke me.

In Jesus name, Amen.

We always hear "let it go" and often respond, "that's easier said than done". The truth is, we do have a choice in what we hold on to and what we let go. Letting go is a choice. You and I can decide what we give power to and what we allow to have authority in our lives. Letting go of our old ways, in our pain, and in our hurts, allows us to replace negative energy with positive energy. Once you decide to finally let go, you release yourself from bondage. In addition to freeing yourself mentally and emotionally, you give way to healing and no longer hide behind the broken pieces of who you used to be.

Letting go takes time, dedication, and work. You must be willing to want change and then allow yourself to channel through all the people and situations that hurt you. I wrote a letter to every person that hurt me and described what they did to me to channel my hurt. One person's letter was twelve pages long. At the end of every letter I wrote, "I forgive you. " Although these people never read the letters, in the end it wasn't for them, it was for me.

Holding on to pain and heartache was suffocating me and I didn't realize it. Alternatively, writing letters freed me and released me from the anger, rage, and bitterness I built inside of me over the years. I was finally able to push it out my system, so the memories and nightmares could stop replaying in my head. When I finished all the letters, I remember praying and asking God to teach me how to forgive instantly, and He led me to Matthew 18:21-22. Being raised by my grandmother, the Bible was always a source of reference, guidance and great stories to compare my life battles.

In this Bible scripture Peter asks Jesus, "Lord, how many times shall I forgive my brother or sister who sins against me? Up to seven times? " Jesus answers, "I tell you, not seven times, but seventy-seven times. " The revelation revealed to me that the "times" in the text is a metaphor for processing the offense either for long term or short term, but it must be forgiven.

Everybody has been extended the same amount of grace offered to us by Christ. It should be noted that, even though I have a repented heart, doesn't mean everybody else does. For this reason, in God's eyes, the umbrella of grace was for me and for everybody that hurt me as well. I had to learn how to forgive for me, not for them.

Will I ever forget? No, but I'm no longer living in prison or bondage centered to that pain. I'm no longer holding on to it intentionally and allowing it to fester inside me causing damage. I chose to let go to live more abundantly. When I chose to let go, I gave God full permission to come into my life and show me the way I should live. He freed me from being consumed by my pain and strengthens me emotionally and spiritually.

"For I consider that the sufferings of this present time are not worthy to be compared with the glory which shall be revealed in us. For the earnest expectation of the creation eagerly waits for the revealing of the sons of God. For the creation was subjected to futility, not willingly, but because of Him who subjected it in hope; because the creation itself also will be delivered from the bondage of corruption into the glorious liberty of the children of God."
Romans 8:18-21

Letting go is the responsibility of what I can do for myself. It's about what I must drop to gain. It's about why it no longer serves me purpose. Today, I can gladly choose to let go and let God. Letting go allows us to dump the baggage and make room for the newness of God. When we choose to let go, God begins to fill us up with the overflow of life's precious gifts. However, it's a choice that we must make daily and we must be intentional about it. You can't just let go once; this is an act of self-love you must keep practicing for the rest of your life.

Let it Go

Let go of every form of hurt, jealousy, envy, resentment, false lies and false assumptions in Jesus name so you can enter into the abundance in which He promised you in this life!

- What do you need to let go of?
- What do you expect from those who hurt you?
- Did you do more harm to yourself by holding on to past hurts?
- What positive outlook can you see from letting go?
- In what ways have you tried to let go of your past and your pain?
- Can you write a letter to everyone who hurt you and not give it to them?
- Can you forgive them?
- Are you making up excuses why you can't move forward?
- Why are you still trying to understand why they did what they did?
- Is it necessary for you to have a reason to let go?
- Letting go means you surrender. Do you want to surrender?
- Can you let go to receive the blessing that's about to blow your mind on the other side?

Let it Go

Use this space to answer the questions from above.

Let it Go

Let it Go

Let it Go

Dear God,

As you stretch me into the one you have called me to be, help me to see my scars and release the offense of anyone who meant to harm me and the times I harmed myself. Teach me how to forgive and love those who you have called me too. Show me thy right hand that I may be obedient to your spirit when you tell me to forgive and let go of those who trespass against me. Lord don't allow me to forfeit the blessing you have on the other side. Wreck my stubbornness and my pride as I cast my cares on you.

In Jesus name, Amen.

Abandonment

Being placed in my grandmother's care was a very eye-opening experience for me. I remember breathing in at a young age of eleven, "ok this is my new reality". Having experienced abused, I felt like my childhood was stripped from me at the age of seven. I no longer functioned as a kid because I was exposed to grown up behavior too soon, I processed life before my time. Regardless of how I wanted to be, and desired to be with my mother and sisters, I had to accept that my mother would never choose me over her husband. Altogether, that was a hard truth that crushed my spirit for years.

When abandonment creeps in, you must remember that it's on an evil assignment from the enemy to steal your peace and joy. Abandonment can also be a form of anxiety. When you experience traumatic loss, in my case the loss of being with my family, you start having trust issues and feelings of fear, thinking that everything is going to be taken away from you.

Being abandoned put me in a dark place. The enemy knew I would always search for answers in things, and fight for them no matter how bad of a situation they kept me in. Many times, I even thought if I never would have said anything, and just kept allowing my mother's husband to molest me, then maybe the relationship between my mother and I would have been saved. I kept thinking that one day, no matter what, my mother was going to get me. When that day never came, the feeling of being rejected broke me. My soul was crushed well into my adult years, from that one moment of abandonment it pierced me with a lifetime thorn.

Abandonment is a thief but staying in alignment with God will help you see past it. When retracing your abandonment issues, pray, and ask God to show you what He's protecting you from. Find peace in knowing that God was protecting you from something perhaps far worse than what you were experiencing. God is for us and He loves us. Instead of thinking about how he took something from you, think about how he replaced it with something better.

Abandonment

God can take any negative thing and turn it into a positive. Even though I felt like I lost time with my mother and sisters, I gained something greater with my grandmother. Authentic love. Abandonment could be God's way of compensating with what they couldn't give you. What He needed you to have and He sent it through the love of someone else. Don't get me wrong, abandonment hurts, but sometimes it can take you out of your traditional way of thinking and allow you to see yourself blessed in an unconventional way. Forcing you to see yourself as a miracle and not broken.

I never desired to live with my grandmother, and I had no choice. Alternatively, I realized it was the best gift my mother could've given me. The enemy wanted to derail me from my destiny, but God stepped in and allowed me to use all that pain for His testimony and to transform my pain into purpose.

"But now, this is what the Lord says—he who created you, Jacob, he who formed you, Israel: "Do not fear, for I have redeemed you; I have summoned you by name; you are mine. When you pass through the waters, I will be with you; and when you pass through the rivers, they will not sweep over you.

When you walk through the fire, you will not be burned; the flames will not set you ablaze. For I am the Lord your God, the Holy One of Israel, your Savior; I give Egypt for your ransom, Cush[a] and Seba in your stead. Since you are precious and honored in my sight, and because I love you, I will give people in exchange for you, nations in exchange for your life.

Do not be afraid, for I am with you; I will bring your children from the east and gather you from the west. I will say to the north, 'Give them up!' and to the south, 'Do not hold them back.' Bring my sons from afar and my daughters from the ends of the earth—everyone who is called by my name, whom I created for my glory, whom I formed and made." Isaiah 43:1-7 (NIV)

Abandonment

No matter what path you walked down, God is still with you. I was stuck in an illusion for a long time, and even my life seemed to be defeated. I've also felt like I've had a wise spirit and mature spirit way before my time. Years of pain caused me to pay closer attention to people and especially to how they treat me.

Going through everything I have in my life; God has given me the gift of having a strong sense of discernment. God was able to turn my abandonment around, as painful as it was. It gave me different spiritual gifts that have allowed me to cope better and help others cope. I thought I lost, but God showed me the advantage of what I gained. The enemy fed me insecurities, but God gave me security. Understand that we all grow through difficult times, but trust that what's meant for evil God will make it good for your.

As you answer these questions healing will take place. Understand that all things work together for the good of those called according to His purpose, and you are called to His purpose. So, no matter the obstacle or trials God only see's you as a winner in His eyes.

- Who/what left you broken?
- Do you think they meant it?
- Do you think they understand what they did?
- How long has this been hurting you?
- Did you blame God?
- Can you make peace with your heart about being abandoned/feeling lost?
- What are some things you hold on to?
- What are some things you need to leave?
- If you could talk to the person who you feel abandoned you, what would you say?
- What good can you see having been abandoned?
- Can you forgive yourself for thinking you are not enough?
- Who can you talk to that can help you realize your worth?

Abandonment

Use this space to answer the questions from above.

Abandonment

Abandonment

Abandonment

Dear God,

Help me with my discernment and allow me to see who is for me and who is against me. I thought certain people were supposed to love me, but instead they put me in a dark place. Deliver me from this dark place and help me realize I am in your divine care. Help me realize how you've picked me up and are carrying me into wholeness. Lord help me to forgive myself and I ask that you forgive me for thinking that you left me. I know now what your word says that you will never leave nor forsake me is a promise to lean on. Help me see that you are working everything for my good. Lord arrest every thought of abandonment in my mind. Use it for your Kingdom glory. Kill the blood line of abandonment that tried to kill me and release my family from any abandonment generational curses.

In Jesus name, Amen

Prayer & Fasting

I never heard my grandmother pray but I remember her always saying, "Netta you better pray!" And to be honest, I really didn't know what prayer looked like. I thought you just prayed when you were in trouble, but I soon learned that prayer was a strategic tool to help me make it through life. I used to love writing in my diaries as a kid, and I would write in them all the time for fun. My diaries were my Bible.

When I first arrived at my grandmother's house, I needed an outlet to say what I couldn't say out loud. Writing became that entry point for me to escape and imagine. As I got older, I realized I had been talking to God my whole life. Those diary entries were my prayers. Those were my love letters, venting sessions, dark secrets being revealed that were only addressed to God.

I could never tell people the stuff I wrote about, but I always felt safe to tell God everything. I'm the type of person who confesses the truth no matter what. I will admit and repent quickly because I am aware of what God wants and that's the kind of heart that He can trust. When God knows that I trust Him, then He in return, trusts me. No matter what I've gone through, I've always relied on prayer to get me through. From experiencing trauma as a child, to an adult living as a loyal addict to toxic behaviors and broken love cycles, prayer has always been my sound connection to God.

As an adult, I have an extremely diligent prayer life. My alarm clock is set to pray five times a day just so I can make sure I encounter God. Prayer should be often and constant. It's the one line of communication that should never be cut off.

Prayer is the place where God hears your heart and the place where He tells you to be quiet to receive His direction. Prayer is the place where discipleship is formed and where waiting on the Lord doesn't take so long because you've inquired Him for all the solutions to whatever you're going through. It's the one place you get to be a child even as an adult. I encourage you to trust God today. Pray, tell him everything and ask Him to rest your mind in His care. Talk to Him as a friend and call Him "ABBA" (God is Father)!

Prayer & Fasting

Prayer isn't something that one should do casually, it should be intentional. Prayer is the most powerful weapon we have to communicate with God. It is the ultimate healing tool you need to make it through life! We are not equipped to handle life alone without the creator's internal guidance. Prayer is the only entrance that we as individuals have as a gift in this world to bring down spiritual establishment here on earth. It is where our human nature and spiritual being come to God. It is the mirror of the Holy Trinity actively operating in your life.

The Trinity consist of God the Father, The Son and The Holy Spirit. The Father is who you acknowledge in prayer as you go before Him. The Son is who you are in the flesh (Human) as you approach God in prayer. The Holy Spirit is the force interceding on your behalf as an access point to the spiritual realm of what you cannot see. Prayer is the delight of the Lord and a weapon to kill warfare before it gets to you on this journey of life. Prayer is a prophecy for your future.

Fasting is a practice that helps us discipline our lives. These both go hand in hand. Fasting is sacrificing anything that has consumed your time, entices your sinful nature, and will cause you to neglect your natural state of mind. Fasting forces you to see the habits that are standing in the way of you flourishing here on earth. Fasting presents us with an internal view of ourselves.

I started fasting the wrong way. I thought I was fasting for God to do what I need him to do in my life. I quickly found out that fasting was revealing what I needed deliverance from. Fasting made me aware of my own demons. Oh, how ugly they were! As a result, I literally became physically sick the more I became aware of what had a hold on my identity for so long. Fasting prompts discipline to focus on what you need to pursue as it relates to your purpose and destiny.

Prayer & Fasting

In Scripture Jesus gives us an example about prayer and fasting, In Mark 9:29 (KJV), it says "So He said to them, "This kind can come out by nothing but prayer and fasting. " At times, you will need to do both!

Although people like our family and friends mean well, they can't help us how God can help us. We wrestle with so many thoughts, experiences, and hurt that only the Father can help us escape them and bring us through. Life can be scary, and the enemy has forces and dark spirits waging war against you. I've encountered demonic forces and supernatural experiences firsthand, and I can't explain every detail to everybody.

People tend to shun spiritual encounters but somehow love to ask spiritual people to pray for them. They either don't know what to say to help me or don't believe me. So, I must go to the source of everything: God. God answers our prayers and uses that line of connection to open our eyes to both light and darkness. When you call on the name of Jesus things happen in this natural world. We are all living a human experience, prepared for a spiritual, eternal life beyond what we can see.

"But Jesus often withdrew to lonely places and prayed. " Luke 5:16

"Therefore, confess your sins to each other and pray for each other so that you may be healed. The prayer of a righteous person is powerful and effective. " James 5:16

"And pray in the Spirit on all occasions with all kinds of prayers and requests. With this in mind, be alert and always keep on praying for all the Lord's people." Ephesians 6:18

Prayer taught me how to vent to God because at the end of the day, He is the only one who can help me with my issues.

Prayer & Fasting

Don't be afraid to pray. It's ok to tell God, "I don't know who I am, but you do because you created me! Tell me who I am! " I know it sounds bold, but that was my prayer and let me just say, when He answered I was blown away. Prayer is a conversation with God, but the experience of being in His presence is far greater than anything you can ever imagine.

Once you have established a planned prayer life and are mature in who you are called to be, your prayers will go from long prayers to short intimate conversations simply saying, "Lord Thy will be done here on earth as it is in heaven Amen." Once you build a solid foundation in seeking God for your life and strengthen your faith in his will, you'll notice how your prayers will go from serving self to extending to people all over the world.

After you answer the questions below, I challenge you to set an alarm on your phone to make time for God. Talk to him seven days a week, five times a day and watch what He does in your life.

1st Alarm: Praise and Thanksgiving (Give Him praise and thanksgiving for His goodness and mercy.)

2nd Alarm: Repentance (Ask Him for forgiveness and for the Holy Spirit to guide you into truth.)

3rd Alarm: Direction (Ask for guidance in your life and allow His word to be a lamp unto your feet.)

4th Alarm: Vision (Ask Him for discernment and to open your eyes to see what He needs you to see.)

5th Alarm: Relationships (Pray for your relationship with Him and with others.)

Prayer & Fasting

- Do you pray?
- How often do you pray?
- Do you know what you need to pray for?
- After you pray how do you feel?
- Has anyone taught you how to pray?
- Do you know what to ask God in prayer?
- Do you have praying friends?
- Do you pray with other people?
- List the people in your life you want to pray for and their needs.
- Do you believe prayer changes things?
- Can you commit to a dedicated life in prayer?

Prayer & Fasting

Use this space to answer the questions from above.

Prayer & Fasting

Prayer & Fasting

Prayer & Fasting

Dear God,

Show me how to pray. Show me what to say. I can't put into words what I need and where I'm going. Please guide me and show me the way. I want to see pass my current life circumstances and into the plans you have already called me to fulfill for my future. God show me who you created me to be so I can be her. I need her and she needs me. I long to see the masterpiece you have called of me. Holy Spirit I long to have a divine encounter with you. Walk me from this nonchalant spirit and guide my steps. Give me direction and be a lamp unto my feet. Lord teach me how to tell my testimony for my good and for your glory. Lord I thank you for opening doors for me, enlarging my territory and I patiently await the growth and change you have for me.

In Jesus name, Amen.

In the Bible, Jesus says this is the model prayer for those that do not know how to pray, what to say or who need an understanding.

The Lord's Prayer
Pray then like this: *"Our Father in heaven, hallowed be your name. Your kingdom come, your will be done, on earth as it is in heaven. Give us this day our daily bread, and forgive us our debts, as we also have forgiven our debtors. And lead us not into temptation but deliver us from evil." Matthew 6:9*

Listen to Yourself

The one person that I didn't trusted was myself. I couldn't trust myself because I didn't know myself. For a long time, I thought I was a mistake. I believed everything negative that was spoken over my life and I replayed those destructive voices in my head for years. Those negative words grew more powerful as time passed and eventually became louder than the voice of God because I was bathed in brokenness.

I eventually learned that I had to listen to myself. Listen to that small inner voice to understand me and who I was. I needed to know why I thought the way I thought and did what I did. At an early age I was introduced to therapy which was a way for me to open and realize I can be fixed. As I've continued to grow and mature, I've become sensitive to my emotions. I care how I'm being treated and I'm vocal about it. I know when I'm being taking advantage of and I call it out.

I'm also at a place when I know, it's time to call my therapist and seek treatment so PTSD and depression won't catch me off guard. Living this new way of life does not mean that all those elements of turmoil are totally gone. I lived in those cycles of brokenness for over 20 years, and it will probably take a lifetime of constant effort of dedication in bettering myself before it's just a memory. However, I pray for it to be my testimony and not my constant fight.

From a young child to now, I have always been a spiritual person. Faith has always been a big part of who I am and throughout my life. Undoubtedly, it's the only part that has kept me sane. Before I knew the realness and truthfulness of faith, I was so intrigued by it. I've always seen things from a Biblical perspective, rather from day to day or in the natural and supernatural. I would see myself as having a psychological experience in the natural world, but I had warfare in the supernatural world.

The Bible says we don't fight against flesh and blood, but against powers and principalities. So, when I thought of my life experiences through the lens of spiritual warfare, I received more revelation about why my mind was in a constant state of confusion.

Listen to Yourself

As I matured in my faith, I started to discern people and understanding the vibe and energy they were giving off. It took time for me to see that the Holy Spirit was alerting me about the spirit of the people I was surrounding myself with. I knew I felt some type of way around certain people, but I didn't understand the depths of it. I thought I was being mean or standoffish, and thought it was just my conscience, my keen sense, or my vibe. Yes, it was that, but even more so, it was the Holy Spirit speaking to me.

God gave everything living a sense of something. A guide to be guided from within. Animals have an instinct that allows them to sense danger and alerts them to prey. As humans we have a conscience and a mind, and the unique gift of thinking. God gives us our intuition as a wonderful gift. After being heartbroken from my mother, father, two abusive relationships, and countless other people, I now understand the importance of listening to myself and listening to God.

I've seen many of things in my life, but I often ignored them because I couldn't distinguish the lies from the truth. After being divorced and sitting in an empty house, I was forced to face the uncomfortable silence of my own breathing. For the first time I could hear my thoughts clearly. Sadly, I didn't recognize my own voice. I didn't know what I wanted to do for me. *What did I like to eat or how to let go of my routine of catering to a marriage?*

Soon after spending time with God, I came to know myself through Him. I stopped ignoring the voices inside and started paying more attention to it. Once I started listening to it and obeying it, I realized how appointed and anointed I am by God. When God speaks, He is a gentle father. He knows what I have endured so He would never make His voice relate to my past hurts. I had to change even my knowledge of what I knew about God and seriously read His word for my life.

Listen to Yourself

God has taken the brokenness of me and not only made me whole but called me to lead those like me. I traded in my will for His good and perfect will. More capable and very equipped to hear Him in me. To be guided with a balance of normalcy to help others come to Christ. In my own unique way.

"Those who live according to the flesh have their minds set on what the flesh desires; but those who live in accordance with the Spirit have their minds set on what the Spirit desires. The mind governed by the flesh is death, but the mind governed by the Spirit is life and peace. The mind governed by the flesh is hostile to God; it does not submit to God's law, nor can it do so. Those who are in the realm of the flesh cannot please God. " Romans 8:5

When you're unsure of who you are, you live in a constant state of confusion. Your mind is so warped from normalizing dysfunction that you eventually learn how to sort it out and rationalize it. The sad reality is that you have never really discovered the real you. You've been so busy replacing that one thing we need God for.

Ask God to show you yourself through His eyes. Starting today, listen to that inner voice. Trust your gut always. That's what I call a Holy Ghost belly experience!

Noah looked crazy until the rain came. Jesus was sleeping on a pillow in the storm on the boat. The lady with the issue of blood believed that 12 years of bleeding would be healed by just one touch at the hem of His garment. They all trusted what was inside of them to keep them in righteous pursuit after God's heart. You have Gods heart. Listen to it while it's still beating. The rhythm of your heart is God's timeline attached to your body. Times up when your heart stops beating.

Listen to Yourself

- What was something you told yourself not to do and you did it anyway?
- Can you trust yourself?
- Are you loyal to yourself?
- What has been your longest time being alone?
- When you make decisions, are you anxious?
- What is something that has altered your thinking?
- Are you confident in yourself?
- What do people say about you?
- What are some boundaries you have in place that you will not go against?
- Can you say "NO" comfortably, and without feeling remorseful?
- Do you know your strengths and weakness?
- Can you take compliments?

Listen to Yourself

Use this space to answer the questions from above.

Listen to Yourself

Listen to Yourself

Listen to Yourself

Dear God,

God allow those that have an ear hear. I want to be sensitive to your word. I want the Holy Spirit in my life, so the spirit of God can lead me. I want to be clear about your direction, wise to what you confirm, and obedient to your ways despite my wants and needs because you know more than I do. Help me trust what you have placed in me because you have great works to do.

In Jesus name, Amen

I used to think I was crazy for talking to myself like I do, until I found out many people do it too! I would be walking around, just having a conversation with myself and God, no different than if I were talking with you. The Bible says we are made in His image and likeness, so I see myself through Him and walking with Him. It really is a profound experience to have a conversation with yourself. I believe that's how you discover who you really are. Can you stand your own quirky, unique and peculiar ways? It's called self-awareness.

After accepting the fact that God created me for real for real, I started to see myself as He saw me. I started reading the Bible more and more. After being addicted to toxic relationships and perversions, I had to find a way to stray from things that would distract me from a relationship in Him. Anything that I put in place of Him, I had to remove. My relationship with Him comes first.

It got to the point where I stopped fighting with my own voice in my head and began seeking God and what He wanted for me. I would be riding in the car with someone else and ask myself, "God who is this person in my life? Reveal their impact in my life. " I made it a point that I would establish clear boundaries with people. I no longer wanted to be led by misplaced vulnerability, and familiarity. I am determined to run everything by God in prayer.

I live in a child-like state so he can always direct me. I've accepted the fact that my mother and father couldn't be the parents I desired them to be, but realized God was the only parent I needed to make it in this chaotic world. I've written letters to God. I've made songs about our relationship. I've learned to fall in love with my first love. After years of replacing Him with things I thought I needed and wanted, and saw how my life never lined up, I realized then how much joy I truly desire from Him.

Seek God

"He that dwelleth in the secret place of the most High shall abide under the shadow of the Almighty. I will say of the Lord, He is my refuge and my fortress: my God; in him will I trust." Psalm 91:1

I figured the best thing for me to do was to live a saved life. Not that old religious life we have been accustom to where nobody changes, but a genuine faith life. A saved life where I don't participate in things that my Heavenly Father hasn't sent instructions for me to do.

I've learned to walk away with full confidence and not act in desperation. I walk in spirit and in truth. I own every right to my failures, bruises, and misfortunates, but also success. That's the freedom God wants all his children to have. Especially his daughters! He wants us to spend time dwelling in His secret place, under His arms, in His shelter and refuge. He'll reveal us in His timing for people to see how someone who was a mess in the world can turn around and be used as a miracle to heal.

- Do you know how to seek God? And hear when he's speaking?
- Do you know the promises He offers?
- Do you read your Bible?
- Do you meditate?
- Do you journal?
- Are you willing to heal?
- Are you dedicated to finding out who God has called you to be?
- Have you accepted what has happened to you?
- Are you accountable to yourself?
- Can you own your flaws? And forgive yourself?
- Are you ready to live free from shame?
- Will you continue to better yourself for the rest of your life?

Seek God

Use this space to answer the questions from above.

Seek God

Seek God

Seek God

Dear God,

Help to understand that you are my first love and nothing else even matters. Help me to know that your desire is to walk and talk with me and lead me down the path of righteousness for your namesake. Help me to see that when I abide in you, you abide in me, and that whatsoever I ask in Your Name I shall receive. I thank you that we have a give-give relationship where I seek ye first the kingdom of God and all these things shall be added unto me for your namesake. Knowing that you want to bless me because I represent you in all thy ways.

In Jesus Name, Amen

Surviving so many things that almost killed me mentally, spiritually, and physically; I believe now more than ever that I am, a divine creation and a miracle. Yes, I have a wild imagination, but I think that's God's way of allowing me to explore that little girl I never got a chance to be.

On this level of life, I believe that everything that happens to me is a God encounter. I fought many times. Lost many opportunities. Had too many heartbreaks. But no more! I believe that now is the time I do the will of God because that's how I stay delivered from a broken lifestyle. I don't see me as perfect, but I do see me as God's beloved.

Choosing to live whole does not mean I will not suffer, it just means I won't let anything stop me from doing what God places on my heart to do. I live whole now because I understand the gifts, He's given me. I was so broken, and cut so deep, but now I know and understand that God was the only doctor in the sick room who could heal me and restored me using my broken parts.

I live whole because I now understand that I have a purpose. My mother and father were just a part of the planning process for God to get me into this life. Only God can take me to higher heights from here on out. I live whole because Jesus took His stripes for me on Calvary and the least I can do is the greater works He's called me to.

I live whole because when people hate me, God reveals them to me and removes them from my life, while protecting me. I live whole knowing God has allowed me to work on me by living through Him. I've gained skills for purpose. I read His word for direction. I center myself around the elders and I confess my sins often to a trusted circle. I live whole because being broken ain't cute.

I live whole knowing I have enough of His Word in me that shall sustain every vibration of wealth coming my way. I live whole knowing that I have a divine right to the kingdom of God.

Once I accepted Jesus Christ as my personal Lord and Savior, my past hurts and mistakes only confirmed what He suffered on the cross. Christ sealed the deal on the cross when he switched places for a girl like me. What He did for me was nothing I could have done for Him. So, I owe Him my best effort to do miraculous things. Just like Jesus rose from the grave; I rose from my brokenness, dusted my shoulders off and promised to keep it pushing.

I live whole because I serve a Holy God and I am a joint heir with Christ Jesus.

"But remember, dear friends, that the apostles of our Master, Jesus Christ, told us this would happen: "In the last days there will be people who don't take these things seriously anymore. They'll treat them like a joke, and make a religion of their own whims and lusts. " These are the ones who split churches, thinking only of themselves. There's nothing to them, no sign of the Spirit!

But you, dear friends, carefully build yourselves up in this most holy faith by praying in the Holy Spirit, staying right at the center of God's love, keeping your arms open and outstretched, ready for the mercy of our Master, Jesus Christ. This is the unending life, the real life!

Go easy on those who hesitate in the faith. Go after those who take the wrong way. Be tender with sinners, but not soft on sin. The sin itself stinks to high heaven.

And now to him who can keep you on your feet, standing tall in his bright presence, fresh and celebrating—to our one God, our only Savior, through Jesus Christ, our Master, be glory, majesty, strength, and rule before all time, and now, and to the end of all time. Yes!" Jude 17-25 (MSG)

You may not serve the God I serve. You may not understand what I wrote. However, we can find the commonality in our life's story. The fact of being broken is the ultimate force that pulled you towards this book. You may not have a relationship with Christ like I do and that's okay, for your walk is in its beginning steps. But at some point, we all must decide to live a whole life. That is our free will gifted by God.

Life has been hard for all of us, but life gets better with a daily dose of reading the Word and saying a prayer for a renewed mind. We no longer toggle in brokenness going forward. So please do everybody a favor that's rooting for you, get better!

Join a church that speaks to your heart. It will not be a perfect place because other broken people are there just like you. Get a medically certified therapist from your cultural background. Join a small group or Bible study. And please don't forget to enjoy the journey!

YOU and ME are designed and created to be WHOLE!

- What about this book has had an impact on you?
- Will you use the prayer concept?
- Will you give it your best to honor God with your life?
- Will you refer this book to another woman?
- Will you make a review about this book?
- Will you join the Authors Facebook group to discuss more about living whole?

Live Whole

Use this space to reflect on what you've learned about yourself and what steps you will take going forth to live whole.

Live Whole

Live Whole

Confession of Faith

I, _____, (insert your name) from this day,_____, (today's date) choose to accept all that has happened to me. I, _____(insert your name) choose to live whole. Trusting that God will work out all things for my good, but for His glory. I surrender my will to be right and I humble myself to get connected to the body of Christ to help me grow in my faith.

I will no longer deny what Jesus did for me on Calvary. I will practice living righteous daily. I will set my eyes on the cross. I will wake up in the morning and reject my fleshly desires and ask God, "What can I do for your kingdom today." I will not be ashamed of my story. I will laugh. I will seek help. I will enjoy the relationships with those who desire one with me. I will trust my instincts. I will not compare where I've been to where I'm going. I will live on purpose with purpose.

Although the enemy will try to come after me, I know that victory is already won for me. I don't have to fight; I will instead call on the name of Jesus to handle my battles. I walk in dominion and power. Who is the King of Kings and Lord of Lords? Jesus! And on Christ, my solid rock I stand. I am God's elite.

AMEN!

About the Author

About the Author

Whenever I'm asked to talk about myself, I usually shy away from the topic. Mainly because, I'm so relatively blunt, that sometimes it scares people. But I'm very observant, funny and sociable. I love dancing, laughing, and traveling. And more than anything, I love seeing people escape from the pains of their life and blossom into a beautiful flower.

I believe in multiple chances because we all fall short. I believe in forgiveness and the realization that my forgiveness doesn't mean I'm obligated to have a relationship with you. I'm a peacemaker, even when it costs me. I believe in seeing the good in people despite their past, while hoping for the same in return.

Far from perfect, I am goal-driven, and vision led. I believe deep in my heart that all things are possible for those (me) who believe, and I lack nothing. After years of suffering with chronic depression, I know now that I am a masterpiece striving to live a life of abundance. I have completely surrendered to God's perfect will for my life. I have a vivid imagination and a God complex of creativity.

I'm a mother to a brilliant and creative young man. I was raised by grandmothers, whom I now call my guardian angels. I'm the eldest of six girls but have a host of sisters in the kingdom of God.

Through trials, pain, and setbacks, that eventually met joy, peace and victory, I am now confident to say that I am Antwoinette: A woman, warrior, mother, friend, sister, and worshiper. And more importantly, I am God's elite!

Daily Confirmations

I Am

- A Child of God (Romans 8:16)
- Redeemed from the hand of the enemy (Psalm 107:2)
- Forgiven (Colossians 1:13&14)
- Saved by Grace through Faith (Ephesians 2:8)
- Justified (Romans 5:1)
- Sanctified (1 Corinthians 6:11)
- A New Creature (2 Corinthians 5:17)
- Partaker of His Divine Nature (2: Peter 1:4)
- Redeemed from the curse of the law (Galatians 3:13)
- Delivered from the Powers of Darkness (Colossians 1:13)
- Led by The Spirit of God (Romans 8:14)
- A Son (Daughter) of God (Romans 8:14)
- Kept in Safety Wherever I Go (Psalm 91:11)
- Getting all my needs met by Jesus (Philippians 4:13)
- Casting all my cares on Jesus (1 Peter 5:7)
- Strong in the Lord and the Power of his might (Ephesians 6:10)
- Doing all things through Christ who gives me strength (Philippians 4:13)
- An Heir of God and a Joint Heir with Jesus (Romans 8:17)
- Heir to the blessings of Abraham (Galatians 3: 13&14)
- Observing and doing the Lord's Commandments (Deuteronomy 28:6)
- Blessed coming in and going out (Deuteronomy 28:6)
- An Heir of Eternal Life (1 John 5:11&12)
- Blessed with all spiritual blessings (Ephesians 1:3)
- Healed by His stripes (1 Peter 2:24)
- Exercising my authority over the enemy (Luke 10:19)
- Above only and not beneath (Deuteronomy 28:13)
- More than a conqueror (Romans 8:37)
- Establishing God's word here on earth (Matthew 16:19)

Daily Confirmations

I **Am**

- An Overcomer by the blood of the lamb and the word of my testimony (Revelation 12:11)
- Daily overcoming the devil (1 John 4:4)
- Not moved by what I see (2 Corinthians 4:18)
- Walking by faith and not by sight (2 Corinthians 5:7)
- Casting down vain imaginations (2 Corinthians 10:4&5)
- Bringing every thought into captivity (2 Corinthians 10:5)
- Being Transformed by the renewing of my mind (Romans 12 1&2)
- A Laborer together with God (1 Corinthians 3:9)
- The Righteous of God in Christ (2 Corinthians 5:21)
- An Imitator of Jesus Christ (Ephesians 5:1)
- The Light of the world (Matthew 5:14)
- Blessing the Lord at all times and continually praising the Lord with my mouth (Psalm 34:1)

Connect with Antwoinette

f Visual Movements

t WiseNetta

Instagram @VisualMovements

in Antwoinette Ayers

email Antwoinette@VisualMovements.com

Visual Movements
Antwoinette Ayers
10850 Lincoln Trail
Ste. 16 #10
Fairview Heights, IL 62208

Finally, be strong in the Lord and in his mighty power.

EPHESIANS 6:10 NIV

Journal

Use this space to write your prayers, thoughts, or daily petitions.

Journal

Use this space to write your prayers, thoughts, or daily petitions.

9 781087 936368